THE WARS OF INDEPENDENCE

Contents

Scotland 700 Years Ago

A Golden Age

Seven hundred years ago, Scotland had a strong king called Alexander III. He knew the people in Scotland could only be happy and live in peace if the king ruled well. He had to make wise laws that were fair to everyone and see that they were obeyed. He had to defend his people against their enemies.

The king's seal was fixed to important letters

Find:

◆ the king on his throne. What is he holding?

Which side of the seal shows the king as:

◆ a wise ruler?
◆ a defender of his people?

In Alexander's time Scotland gradually became better off. The country was at peace. The king's **sheriffs** helped to keep law and order. People could live without fear of attack. Later when people looked back on this time they called it a Golden Age.

Alexander's sister was married to Edward I, the powerful king of England. In those days Scotland and England were two separate countries. Find them on the map.

Sheriff

Someone in charge of the king's affairs in an area called a shire.

A map of Scotland and her neighbour England in the 13th century.

Find:
◆ Scotland.
◆ England.

Which country is bigger?

The king's journeys and castles

Alexander III and other Scottish kings had many castles and estates in England as well as in Scotland. Some important nobles had lands and castles in France as well. To eat up the food and supplies **tenants** paid in rent, they moved round from one castle to another. This gave time for the drains in the castle to be cleared once everyone had moved out. As the king journeyed round, the people in the country had a chance to see and know him. He often lived at the castles of great nobles to whom he had given land.

> ### Tenant
> A person who has the use of property or land in return for paying rent.

When the king needed advice or extra money to run the country he would send letters to his nobles and important churchmen telling them to meet him at a particular castle. This is why laws were often made at Stirling, Edinburgh, Perth, Roxburgh and other places.

This wagon could carry people and their belongings from one castle to another.

Find:
- clues that the wagon must be very heavy.
- clues that important people are in the wagon.

When the king built a castle he tried to find a place with a good water supply which would be easy to defend.

An ideal place was on a hill, at a loop in a river or where two rivers met. The castles were wooden towers which could be put up quickly.

This picture shows what was done when there were no hills.

At the Motte of Urr the castle builders made a huge mound of earth called a motte. The courtyard below was called the bailey.

Find:
- the place where the wooden castle would have been built.
- the ditch round the mound.
- the ditch round both motte and bailey.

Why do you think the ditches were made?

Living in a Castle

Stone castles and towers

There was not much room in a small wooden castle. It could easily catch fire. Alexander III and his nobles built stronger stone castles but there were still some wooden ones. The new castles had thick walls and more rooms. Some lairds built single stone towers which cost much less.

Eilean Donan Castle, Ross and Cromarty

Find the strong stone tower.
Why was this a good place
for a castle?

The castle at Dirleton near North Berwick may have looked like this long ago.

Find:

- the high walls round the courtyard. Inside the courtyard the castle well provided water. There were stables, store rooms and workshops.
- the narrow slits in the wall for firing arrows.
- the ditch or moat filled with water round the castle.
- the bridge over the moat. The drawbridge at the entrance could be pulled up to keep out enemies.
- the round towers at the corners of the castle.
- the battlements on top where defenders could look out.

The stone castles were damp and draughty. In Scotland's cold climate open fires were burned in the Great Hall of the castle nearly all year round.

The Great Hall at Doune Castle

Find:

- the fire basket in the centre of the Great Hall.
- the stone walls. Rushes on the stone floor helped to keep out the cold. The lord and his family wore long robes trimmed or lined with fur to keep themselves warm.
- the rafters holding up the wooden ceiling.
- the bench at the side.

There was not much furniture. Servants set up a table for dinner. The lord might have a chair. Other people sat on stools or benches.

Everyone ate in the Great Hall. When the meal was over people stayed in the hall to drink and listen to stories. A travelling minstrel might play his harp and sing songs of brave deeds long ago. Jugglers and musicians often visited. People liked to dance. Everyone held hands and danced round in a circle. The lord might decide to play chess with a guest and call for his chessmen to be brought.

These chessmen from Lewis are carved from walrus ivory.

Find:

- ◆ **the king wearing a crown.**
- ◆ **the bishop holding his staff which looks like a shepherd's crook.**
- ◆ **the knight holding his shield.**

Ladies in the castle

Ladies in the castle were often busy. A lord's wife had to run the castle so that there was always food and other supplies. Most things were made at home. Women preserved fruit in summer for the cold winter months, brewed **ale**, made soap and candles and pickled fresh meat in salt so that it would keep. All the blankets and sheets used had to be made in the castle. Ladies learned to use herbs as medicine to help care for the sick or wounded. If the castle was attacked while the lord was away, his lady took command.

Ladies did a great deal of spinning and weaving as well as embroidery.

Find:

- ◆ **the two ladies preparing wool for spinning.**
- ◆ **the lady spinning with a spindle hanging from her hand.**
- ◆ **the lady in front of a weaving loom.**
- ◆ **clues that these ladies were well off.**

Often women did not choose the person they would like to marry. After a woman married, the things she owned belonged to her husband. Kings and nobles married their children to people whose lands would make them richer or more powerful.

Ale
A drink made from barley.

Spindle
A stick with a notch at the top used to draw out wool for spinning into thread.

Arms and armour

The lord of a castle who had land from the king had to be ready to fight for the king in wartime. He must bring knights and men with him who had the armour and weapons they needed.

The lord only wore armour when he went off to fight. It was very heavy and took quite a while to put on. Knights had **squires** to help.

This is how a knight of 700 years ago might look.

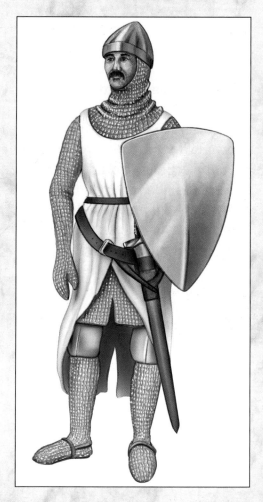

Find:

◆ the suit of chain mail which covers the knight from head to toe. Underneath he wore a padded tunic with long sleeves.
◆ the long sleeveless linen gown which is slit at the back and the front to make riding easier.
◆ gloves made of chain mail which allow the knight to move his hands.
◆ the heavy iron helmet.
◆ the knight's two weapons.
◆ the shield.

It was hard for knights to know one another when they wore their helmets. The shield had a coat of arms painted on it. Everybody knew which coat of arms belonged to which family. Sometimes knights riding into battle had a banner on their spear with the same coat of arms.

Wallace

Douglas

These are two well known Scottish coats of arms.

Squire
Someone who is training to be a knight.

Chain mail
Armour made by joining iron rings together.

Because knights had to keep in training they sometimes had mock battles called tournaments like the one carved on this ivory panel.

Tournaments were fought with real weapons and armour. There were special rules for each contest. All the people in the castle enjoyed watching but sometimes knights were killed or wounded.

Find:

- The two armed knights charging towards each other. What are they trying to do?
- the people looking on. Where are they sitting?
- the trumpeters announcing the start of the contest.
- the castle.
- the two knights kneeling to ask a blessing before the fight.

Everyone living in a castle spent a lot of time in the open air. The king and his nobles enjoyed hunting for wild boar, deer and other animals in the forests and rough waste ground near the castles. This was a good way of getting fresh meat.

Find:

- the huntsman. What is he doing?
- the dogs.
- the hunted stag.
- the other man in the picture. What is he going to do?

Living in the Country

Houses

In Scotland 700 years ago only a few people lived in castles. Most people lived in the country in houses built like the one in this picture.

An old ruined farm cottage in Caithness

Houses had a wooden framework holding up the roof. There was no chimney. A hole in the roof let out smoke and let in light. Often there were no windows. The door was a wooden frame covered with animal skin.

Find:

◆ the tree trunks set opposite each other.
◆ the place where the tree trunks are joined at the top with wooden pegs.
◆ the strong thin branches used to finish the framework.
◆ the turf covering the roof.

> **Turf**
> Earth with the grass and its roots still in it.

Outside their cottages farm folk grew peas, kail and beans.
The picture shows what it was like inside a country cottage
700 years ago.

Find:

- the smoky peat fire with the cut peats stacked beside it.
- the woman making bannocks or oatcakes.
- the man eating porridge from a wooden bowl. What is he wearing? How is the woman dressed? Who do you think made the clothes?
- the beds filled with heather.
- the big iron cooking pot full of broth hanging from the rafters.

- the children sitting beside their grandmother listening to stories of long ago.
- the animals sharing the house. How are they kept apart? Why are they inside the house? How will they help to keep the house warm in winter?

The dung dropped by the animals was spread on the fields. Why do you think this was?

Bannock

A round flat cake made in Scotland from barley or wheat.

Peat

A thick brown layer of rotted down grass and moss found in some parts of Scotland. When it is cut out with a spade and dried it burns well.

Broth

A soup made by boiling meat, barley and vegetables in water.

Work on the land

People lived in small groups of families with their land round about wherever the soil was good. These were called farm touns. Roads were mostly rough tracks and there were only a few rivers which had good bridges. Country people did not travel far from home.

The people in the farm toun helped one another. In spring each family lent its oxen to pull the heavy wooden plough.

Find:

◆ the plough.
◆ the oxen. How many are pulling the plough? When the soil was heavy more oxen were needed.
◆ the man guiding the plough from behind. What is the man in front doing?
◆ the wooden collars called 'yokes' which keep the oxen in pairs. Why was it hard to turn the oxen in the field?

Oxen

Cattle used to pull heavy loads.

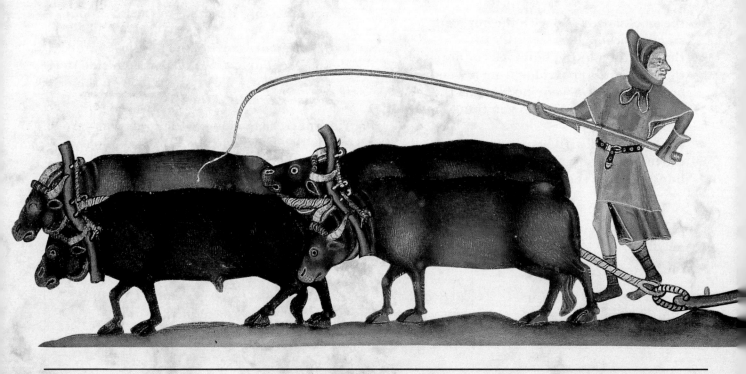

Photographs from the air sometimes give clues about earlier ways of farming.

Home Farm, Wardhouse, Aberdeenshire

Find:

◆ the long strips called rigs on which farmers grew their crops. Each farmer had rigs scattered in different parts of the field so that everyone shared the good land.
◆ round circles which mark the houses of farm workers.
◆ the sloping ground where crops were grown. Often the flat ground was too marshy to grow crops.

In the summer the farmers moved their cattle and sheep to fresh grass on higher ground. The shepherds and cowherds lived in little bee-hive shaped huts called shielings. There the sheep could be sheared and a watch kept for foxes and wolves. The women and children in the toun worked hard. They milked the cows, sheep and goats.

Find:

◆ the woman milking a cow.
◆ the rope used to tie the cow.
◆ the wooden bucket for the milk.

The milk was churned into butter. Sometimes they added some cow hair to the thin milk to help the butter to thicken. They might put a frog to jump about in the churn to make the butter form more quickly.

What other jobs would the farm folk have to do?

Paying rent

The folk in the farm toun did not own the land. It belonged to the **laird** who protected them and they had to pay him a rent as tenants. Some of the rent for the laird was paid in eggs or chickens or part of their crop. Every family had to do certain work for the laird, often at times when they were very busy themselves.

Find:

◆ the men and woman reaping the grain.
◆ the curved tools called sickles they are using to cut the corn.
◆ the laird's overseer who is telling them what to do.

At what other busy times of the year would farm folk have to work on the laird's land?

The laird helped his tenants by allowing them to cut peats and gather kindling for their fires. Their pigs were allowed to feed in the woods.

Find:

◆ the pigs looking for food.
◆ the men beating the trees. Why are they doing this?

Laird	Overseer	Kindling
The owner of land on which tenants stay in Scotland.	Someone who watches other people at work and tells them what to do.	Small twigs and branches of dry wood good for starting a fire.

Living in a Burgh

Why towns grew up

Although most people lived in the countryside 700 years ago, towns had been growing up near important castles or abbeys, or at river crossing places. These towns became burghs when they were given a charter like this one.

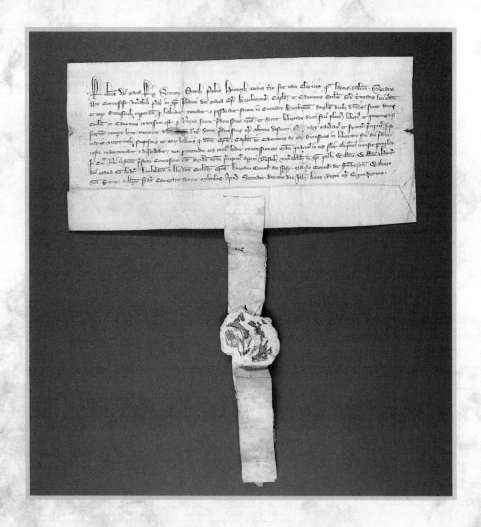

This charter was granted to the royal burgh of Montrose by King David II in 1352.

Like all charters it was written on parchment which is a strong material made from the skin of sheep or goats.

Find:

◆ the Latin writing.
◆ the seal at the end of the charter.

Charter

A special document that explained the rights and duties of the people living in a burgh. Charters were written in Latin.

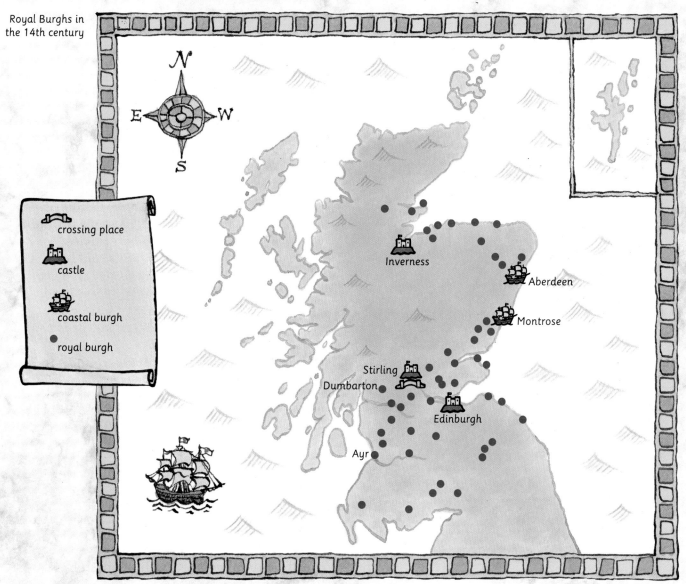

Royal Burghs in the 14th century

crossing place
castle
coastal burgh
royal burgh

Inverness
Aberdeen
Montrose
Stirling
Dumbarton
Edinburgh
Ayr

The Scottish burghs shown on this map have had royal charters for over 700 years.

Find royal burghs:

◆ **on the coast where merchants could send goods abroad.**
◆ **at the mouth of a large river.**
◆ **near an important crossing place.**

Why were these good places to set up new towns?

This is what the king did

✛ invited merchants to come from other countries.
✛ gave them land rent free for a year in the place he had chosen for the town.
✛ let them build houses and shops.
✛ made them special promises in a charter.
✛ gave them the right to hold markets and fairs.

Other powerful people copied the king and gave charters to burghs on their land.

The king knew merchants could become rich selling Scottish fish ,wool, skins, leather and furs in return for fine goods from other countries. Rich merchants paid rent, taxes and **customs duties** to the king.

Customs duties

Money charged on goods coming into a country or leaving it.

Merchants and craftspeople

This is the seal of the town of Burntisland in Fife.

Find:

◆ the merchant ship. Rich merchants sent ships to France, Germany, Holland and other places filled with Scottish cloth, wool, animal skins and hides. The ships brought back wine, raisins, spices, silks and other fine goods which were not made in Scotland.

◆ the three flags on the ship. What shape is the cross?

◆ the thistles round the seal.

What do these clues tell you about Burntisland?

Find:

◆ the man with the wood who is keeping the fire in the furnace hot.

◆ the smith holding some tongs.

◆ the horse shoe in the fire.

Why is the smith using tongs?

Only merchants could trade abroad. Craftspeople made things to sell locally. They were never as rich as merchants. Many craftspeople were smiths who worked with metal. There were goldsmiths, tinsmiths and blacksmiths.

The town plan

A modern artist has used an old plan and other information from letters and charters written 700 years ago to make this map. It shows what a town probably looked like.

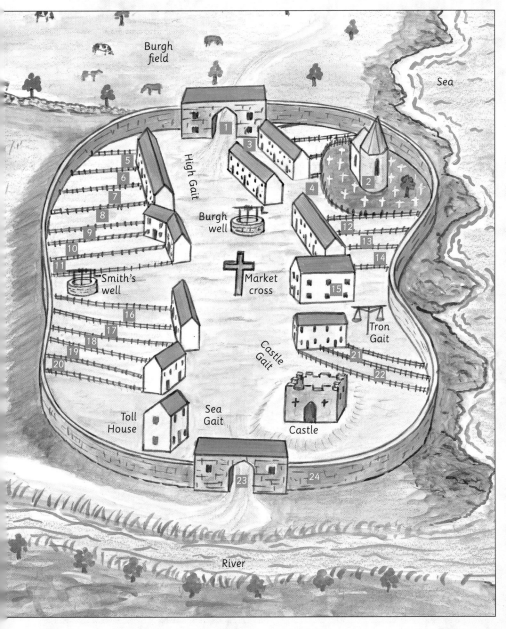

Find:

◆ the walls which protect the burgh.
◆ the entrances to the burgh called ports.
◆ the wooden houses covered with thatch. Fires sometimes spread quickly. Aberdeen was completely burned down in 1244. Why do you think this happened?
◆ the long narrow strips of land behind the houses where the townsfolk had their workshops and stores. What else was this land used for?

Key

1	North Port
2	Church
3	Cow Gait
4	Kirk Gait
5	Robert Smith's land
6	Thomas Saddler's land
7	Allan Dyer's land
8	John Webster's land
9	Candle Wynd
10	Candle Rigs
11	Candle Rigs
12	Adam Miller's land
13	John Fletcher's land
14	William Goldsmith's land
15	Tolbooth
16	John Smith's land
17	Edward Tailor's land
18	Skinner's Gait
19	Thomas Skinner's land
20	Martin The Flesher
21	Robert Smith's land
22	Edward Tailor's land
23	South Port
24	Town Wall

Find:

◆ the castle where the king's sheriff stayed.
◆ the market cross where goods were sold on market day. When fairs were held travelling merchants put up stalls also. Some older burghs still have a fair holiday. For nearly 700 years Glasgow has had a fair in July. There is a Lammas Fair at Inverkeithing and a Trinity Fair near Brechin.
◆ the place where the candlemaker worked behind his house. What other craftspeople worked in the town?
◆ the road which the cowherd took to and from the grassy burgh field. Why did he collect the cows early every morning to spend the day outside the town?
◆ the church (kirk) near the market place.

Thatch
A roof made of straw.

Gait
A street or road.

Religious Life

Going to church

This church at Dalmeny near South Queensferry was built over 700 years ago. On Sundays and Holy days everyone went to church.

Find:

- ◆ the entrance door with a round arch.
- ◆ the windows of the church. What shape are they?

Monks and nuns

The men who are kneeling down in this picture have chosen to serve the church in a special way as monks. For the rest of their lives they will live in a monastery apart from other people.

Find:

◆ the three monks standing at the back. What do you notice about their hairstyle?

◆ the monk with scissors. What is he doing to the man kneeling in front of him?

Why do you think monks cut their hair in a special way?

The women in this picture are called **nuns**. They lived apart from other people in a nunnery. In Scotland a monk called a prior was put in charge of all the money affairs of each nunnery.

Find:

◆ the nuns singing during a service. There were seven services each day including one in the middle of the night.

◆ the choir stalls in which the nuns sat during a service. How are the nuns separated from each other?

◆ the white cloth called a wimpole which each num wore to cover her hair. Both monks and nuns dressed very simply. Find a clue showing what they wore on their feet.

Monks and nuns made three promises when they left their homes and families. They would never marry. They would own nothing for themselves. They would always obey orders in the church.

Nun

A woman who has made promises to live apart from ordinary life in order to serve God.

Scottish kings and great landowners gave gifts of land to the monks. Because the monks knew how to farm well and could read and write, they were very useful to Scotland.

Monks copied out books and wrote important letters. Seven hundred years ago books were written by hand. There was no printing press. Some hand-written books were beautifully decorated with pictures like this one made for the Laird of Arbuthnott.

A page from the Arbuthnott Missal

The church at Arbuthnott in Kincardineshire is called the Kirk of St. Ternan. The priest, James Sibbald, who decorated this prayer book gave the saint the face of an important churchman, the Archbishop of St. Andrews.

Find:

- St. Ternan. How do you think James Sibbald made him look like the Archbishop in charge of bishops and priests?
- the decoration round the picture of St. Ternan. What flowers can you see?
- the picture of the countryside shown through the window. What does it show?

Why do you think books were very precious 700 years ago?

Arbroath Abbey

The monks spent most of their lives in abbeys or monasteries. Some abbeys became very rich and important.

Arbroath Abbey is now a ruin but this picture shows how splendid it must have been long ago. The abbot in charge often gave advice to the king.

A modern artist has painted this picture to show what the abbey probably looked like in the past.

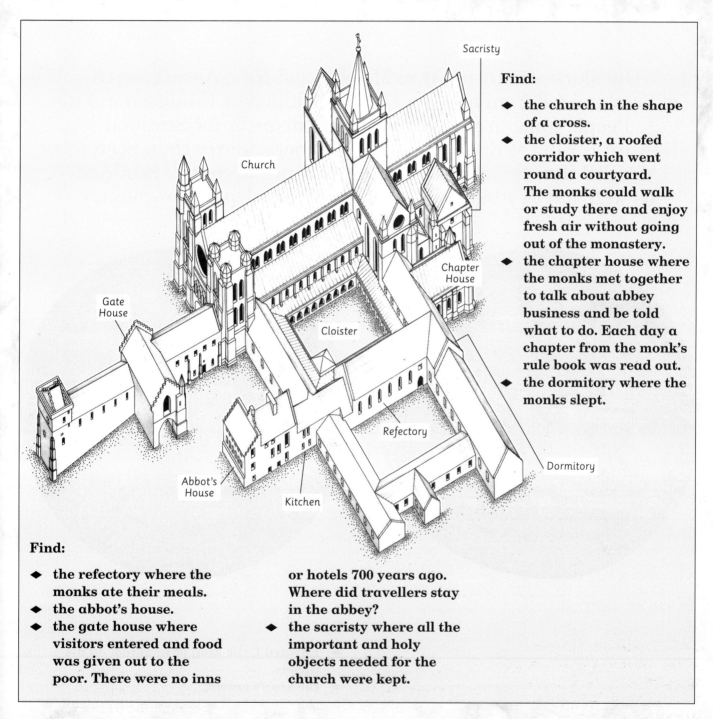

Find:
- the church in the shape of a cross.
- the cloister, a roofed corridor which went round a courtyard. The monks could walk or study there and enjoy fresh air without going out of the monastery.
- the chapter house where the monks met together to talk about abbey business and be told what to do. Each day a chapter from the monk's rule book was read out.
- the dormitory where the monks slept.

Find:
- the refectory where the monks ate their meals.
- the abbot's house.
- the gate house where visitors entered and food was given out to the poor. There were no inns or hotels 700 years ago. Where did travellers stay in the abbey?
- the sacristy where all the important and holy objects needed for the church were kept.

Although the monks ran hospitals and looked after sick people, the abbey hospital is not shown in this picture. Why did monks build their hospitals far away from the other buildings in the abbey?

The Struggle for Independence

The death of the King

One dark stormy night in March 1286 King Alexander III of Scotland fell from his horse and was killed at Kinghorn in Fife. People came to see this as a great disaster for Scotland. Edward I, King of England, a much bigger country than Scotland, decided that this gave him a good chance to control Scotland as well, but Scotland wished to stay an independent country.

The Great Seal of Edward I

Find:

◆ Edward I, the king of England, on his throne.
◆ the king's crown.
◆ the round ball with a cross on top called an orb which shows the king is the ruler of his people.

Independent

Free to decide what to do without having to obey others.

The Maid of Norway

Alexander III left no grown-up son to take over. The new ruler of Scotland was the king's grand-daughter Margaret, a little girl of four who lived in Norway. She was far too young to come to Scotland. The great men of Scotland met at Scone to decide what to do. They chose six guardians, important lords and bishops, to run the country for her.

Edward saw a chance to join Scotland to England without fighting. He arranged that his son, who would be king of England one day, should marry the little queen. The six guardians were pleased but they said that Scotland was to stay a free separate country. They refused to let Edward send English soldiers to take over Scottish castles.

Three years later, in September 1290, Margaret set out from Norway in a ship like this.

The weather was stormy and the seas were rough. Margaret became ill. She died in Orkney without ever seeing her kingdom.

Find:

◆ the sail of the ship.
◆ the rudder on the right hand side which helped to steer the ship.
◆ the steersman beside the rudder. This helps you to see how big the ship was.

Why was the journey from Norway to Scotland a difficult one for a child?

Choosing a king

Scotland was without a ruler. Thirteen men who were relatives of Alexander III each claimed the right to be king of Scotland. The Bishop of St. Andrews was afraid they would begin fighting each other. He decided to write to King Edward I of England to ask him to decide which one should be king. He knew none of them would dare to disagree with such a powerful ruler.

Why did the bishop write to King Edward? Did he ask him to come to Scotland? What did he want him to do?

The kingdom is in trouble.

There is fear of a general war and a great slaughter of men unless Your Majesty acts quickly.

Send soldiers to the Borders to save the shedding of blood.

An artist's drawing of the bishop's letter to Edward I

King Edward agreed to judge which person had the best claim to be king. He came north to meet them at his great castle at Norham on the River Tweed.

The ruins of the great castle at Norham

King Edward saw another chance to take control of
Scotland by claiming that he was the overlord of Scotland.
He told the Scots that they only had their lands because the
English king had granted it in the first place. They had to
obey him just like his English lords.

Some Scottish nobles had lands in England as well as
Scotland. They agreed that Edward was their overlord for
the lands they had in England. Eight of the people who
wanted to be King of Scotland put their seals on this
document which said that Edward I of England was the
overlord of Scotland.

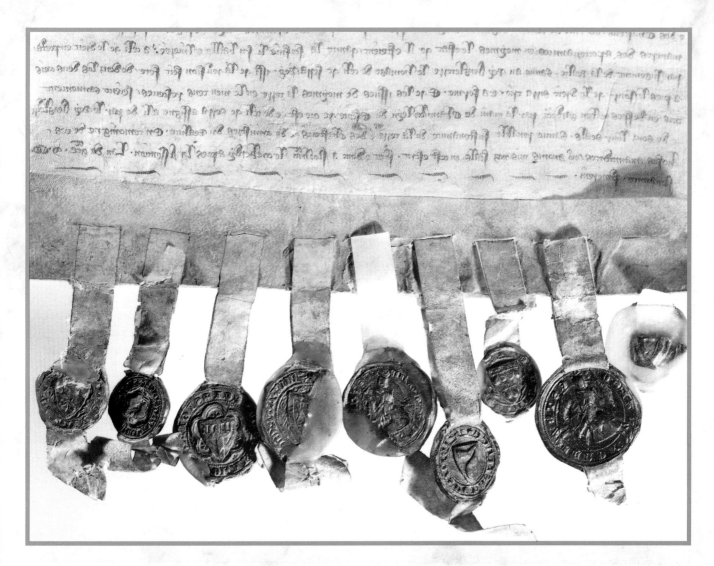

Find:

◆ the seals of the men who promised to accept Edward as
their overlord.

Why were these seals attached to the document?

John Balliol, Toom Tabard

Edward I took time to study the royal family tree of Scotland.

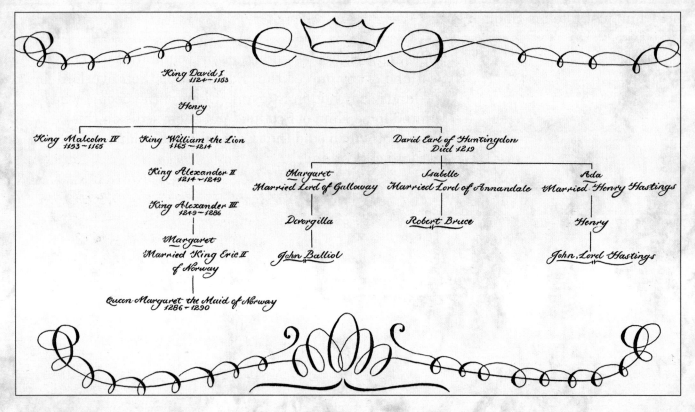

This family tree shows the people descended from King David I.

Find:

◆ **King David from whom the others were descended.**

◆ **Alexander III. How long was he King of Scotland?**

◆ **Margaret, the Maid of Norway. She is the last of the line of rulers descended from King William the Lion.**

◆ **the three descendants of David, Earl of Huntingdon, who each had a claim to the throne.**

Then he chose John Balliol to be the new king.

The next day John Balliol knelt before King Edward as his overlord. He was crowned King John of Scotland at Scone on St. Andrews Day, 1292.

King John's reign lasted only four years. From the start Edward made it clear that he, and not King John, was the real ruler of Scotland. He treated John just like an English noble and not as a king. John was often called to journey all the way to Edward's court in London. Many Scots were unhappy. They called their new king 'Toom Tabard' which means 'empty coat'. They meant that he looked and dressed like a king but could not rule like one.

The invasion of Scotland

In 1294 King Edward of England made a demand the Scots
could not obey. England was at war with France but
Scotland was not. The Scots and the French were friends.
Edward ordered King John of Scotland to bring a large
Scottish army to help him fight against the French.

The Scots refused. Instead they made an agreement with
Edward's enemies in France. This agreement came to be
called The Auld Alliance. It helped both France and
Scotland for many years in their wars against England but
at first Edward took a terrible revenge. Edward did not
want trouble in Scotland when he was fighting France. He
came north with his army to punish the Scots. When he
captured the great Scottish port of Berwick his soldiers
killed men, women and children without mercy and took
everything of value. This is called looting.

This picture shows soldiers looting another
captured city.

Find:

◆ soldiers taking a chest from a house.
◆ soldiers throwing things from the window
   of a house. What kind of goods are they
   stealing?
◆ soldiers drinking jugs of wine. What might
   happen if they drink too much?

Edward's army pushed north through Scotland to the north-east coast. These English silver coins were found at Montrose in Angus. Edward stayed at nearby Brechin Castle for a few days.

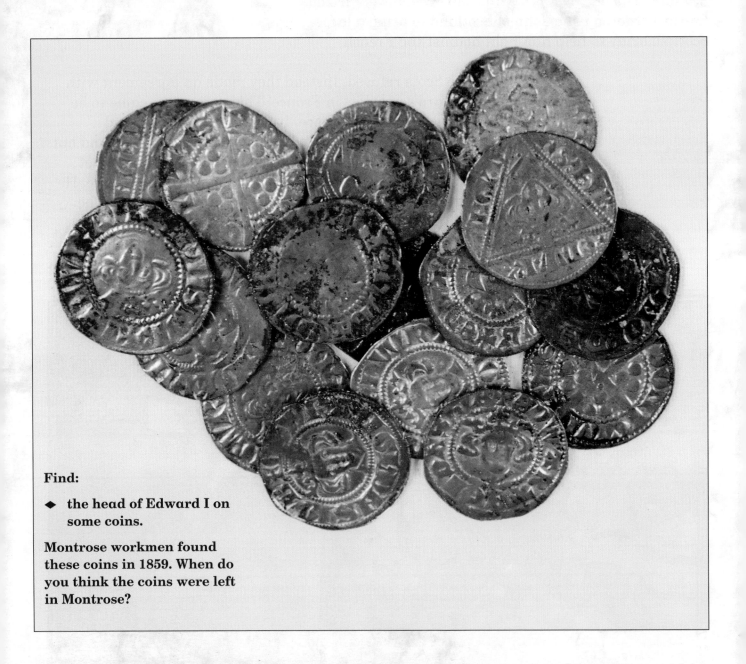

Find:

◆ **the head of Edward I on some coins.**

Montrose workmen found these coins in 1859. When do you think the coins were left in Montrose?

At last King John of Scotland was taken prisoner. Edward did not even bother to see him. John appeared before Edward's men at Stracathro near Brechin. His crown had been taken from him. Humbly dressed, with a white wand in his hand, he gave up the Kingdom of Scotland to Edward of England.

Edward decided to rule Scotland for himself. All the important people in castles, churches and burghs were made to swear a promise to be loyal to King Edward of England. An Englishman was made Governor of Scotland. There were English soldiers, judges, sheriffs and tax collectors everywhere.

Edward took some of Scotland's greatest treasures back to England. The Stone of Destiny on which Scottish kings were always crowned was sent to Westminster Abbey in London. It was put under the English throne and is still there today.

Find:

◆ **the stone under the Coronation Chair.**

Why do you think Edward placed it there?

The Coronation Chair in Westminster Abbey

William Wallace

A new leader

New leaders came forward to drive out the English and bring John Balliol back as King of Scotland.

The greatest of these was William Wallace, a knight's son, who was made an outlaw when he would not promise to be loyal to Edward. This statue of him was put up in Stirling in 1859.

Outlaw

Someone who has no rights because he has been put outside the law for doing something wrong.

Wallace had a special reason to hate the English. He killed an English soldier in a quarrel and in revenge the English burned his house in Lanark and killed his wife. In 1297 Wallace led a small group of thirty men to Lanark. He killed the English sheriff and the English soldiers were driven out of the town. Many ordinary folk joined him after that to fight against the English.

Another young leader, Andrew Murray, whose father and uncle were prisoners of King Edward, drove the English out of castles in the north of Scotland.

This letter was sent by Wallace and Murray to merchants in Hamburg and Lubeck in Germany. It told the mayors of the German cities that it was now safe to trade once more with Scotland since it had been taken back by war from the power of the English.

Why was it important for Scotland to be able to trade with other countries in Europe?

Stirling Bridge

When they learned that a large English army was marching north to deal with them, Wallace and Murray made for the important crossing point at Stirling. They waited on the far side of the wooden bridge which crossed the River Forth.

You can see from this modern picture what happened.

An artist's picture of the Battle of Stirling Bridge

The Scots allowed some English soldiers to cross. Then they charged. The bridge was narrow so that only two knights could cross at a time. The English could not quickly help their soldiers on the other side. Some knights fell in the river and drowned in their heavy armour. Although they were not great nobles,

William Wallace and Andrew Murray won a great victory. Andrew Murray died later of his wounds but Wallace was able to drive the English out of much of Scotland. He became Guardian of Scotland for King John Balliol who was a prisoner in England.

Find:

◆ **Stirling Castle on the high ground behind the bridge.**
◆ **which side the Scots were placed.**
◆ **the English knights who have fallen in the river. How could this have happened?**

Why do you think the English chose to cross this narrow bridge?

The Hammer of the Scots

Edward was not at Stirling Bridge. He was fighting in France but the next summer, in 1298, he came back to Scotland at the head of a great army. He had an important new weapon called the longbow.

Here are soldiers using longbows.

Find:

◆ the archers on the left using longbows. Arrows from a longbow could be fired quickly one after another. They were powerful enough to pierce a knight's armour completely through.
◆ the archer who is winding up the cord of his crossbow to stretch it tightly. This took more time.

Edward decided to use longbows in his battle against the Scots. Wallace came face to face with Edward's army at Falkirk. The Scots were not so well armed as the English. Most Scottish soldiers could only afford simple weapons. Edward's archers killed many Scottish spearmen. The English knights charged and swept the Scots from the battlefield.

In England Edward was called The Hammer of the Scots. What does this mean? Do you think it is a good nickname for Edward?

Although he had lost the battle, Wallace kept on trying to set Scotland free from the English. For five years he caused trouble to English soldiers in different parts of Scotland. More than anything Edward wanted to catch Wallace and make an example of him so that no one else would dare to go against the English rule.

Wallace was in hiding and no one would give him away but at last Wallace was tricked by a Scottish knight, Sir John Menteith. He took Wallace prisoner and handed him over to Edward.

In London Wallace was tried here at Westminster Hall.

Wallace was sentenced to a cruel death after his trial. Why was he not put on trial in Scotland?

Wallace was dragged by a horse through the streets of London to be hanged at Smithfield. His head was stuck on a pole on London Bridge. His arms and legs were cut off and sent as a warning to be shown in Newcastle, Berwick, Perth and Stirling.

The English judges had decided Wallace was a traitor to Edward but all Scots know he was not a traitor to Scotland.

Robert the Bruce

Bruce claims the crown of Scotland

When Wallace died it seemed that Scotland would never be free from England as it had been in the time of Alexander III. Then a new leader appeared with a strong right to be king. He gave up the lands he had in England to fight for Scotland's freedom. His name was Robert the Bruce. This is his statue.

The statue of King Robert the Bruce at Bannockburn

The Bruce family had lands in Scotland and England. Robert the Bruce had not given Wallace a great deal of help because Wallace wanted to bring back John Balliol as King of Scotland. Bruce wanted to be king himself. When Wallace was killed Bruce began to lead the Scots against the English.

Bruce quarrelled with John Balliol's nephew John Comyn in the church at Dumfries. Comyn was stabbed to death. All Comyn's friends and followers in Buchan, Argyll and Galloway were against Bruce from then on. Many church people thought Bruce was a murderer and an enemy of God.

Find:

◆ **Bruce being crowned.**
◆ **the Countess of Buchan on the right with the gold crown.**

What had happened to the coronation seat usually used in Scotland?

Some people wanted Bruce as King of Scotland. He was made king in secret at Scone in March 1306. The Countess of Buchan placed a simple gold crown on his head. Although the Church was against Bruce, the Bishops of Glasgow and St. Andrews were there.

The seal of Scone Abbey shows Bruce being crowned.

Edward I was furious that there was more trouble in Scotland. Robert Bruce was hunted by the English and by Comyn's friends. His little army was beaten at Methven Wood near Perth and he had to go into hiding. King Edward gave Bruce's lands to other people. His wife and twelve year old daughter were put in prison. So were the bishops who had helped him. His sister Mary and the Countess of Buchan were put in iron cages and hung outside the castle walls.

LADY BRUCE, Sister of Robert Bruce King of Scotland, confined in a CAGE & exposed on the Battlements of Roxburgh Castle by order of EDWARD I. King of England.

Find:

◆ **the cage and Mary Bruce.**

Why did Edward order such a cruel punishment?

Capturing castles

Edward had filled the Scottish castles with English soldiers to keep down the Scots. In 1307, when he was leading another army into Scotland, Edward died. His son Edward II, was no a soldier like his father. This gave King Robert the Bruce a chance to deal with his enemies.

This picture shows how soldiers usually attacked a castle 700 years ago.

Find:

◆ the defenders on the battlements of the castle. What are they doing?

◆ the soldiers using different sorts of weapons. How many types of weapon can you see?

◆ the camp for the soldiers who are attacking?

Bruce had no weapons like this. This is how he captured the smaller castles.

• He hid in the hills with his men.
• He made surprise attacks with small groups of men.
• He destroyed each captured castle so that the English could not use it again.

Often a machine which could hurl huge stones at the castle was used.

The Scots attacking Carlisle in 1315.

Find:

◆ the stone attached to the long arm of the machine held down by a rope.
◆ the man who will cut the rope with his axe.
◆ the heavy weight on the end of the beam which will fall when the rope is cut.

What will happen to the stone?

By 1311 Bruce's army had grown strong enough to try to capture the great stone castles where the English soldiers held out. Bruce had to look for the weak places in the castle defences. Often Bruce's men used the points of their spears to hook long rope ladders to the top of a castle wall in the dark. Then they climbed up.

For many weeks Bruce and his men camped beside the River Tay outside the strong stone walls of Perth Castle with its wide deep moat. He pretended to give up and go away. Then one dark wintry night the Scots came back. Led by Bruce they waded up to their necks across the black icy waters of the moat and climbed the walls. The soldiers in the castle were taken completely by surprise.

This picture shows how the Scots captured Linlithgow Castle. A farmer, William Birnie, was delivering a load of hay. There were oxen pulling his cart. He let the oxen go free and the cart was left stuck in the gateway so that the English soldiers could not close the gate. Out jumped eight armed Scots to overpower the guards. The other Scots who had been waiting hidden outside rushed in and captured the castle.

Find:

- ◆ the hay cart blocking the gate.
- ◆ the English troops rushing to fight off the attackers.

Why do you think this plan worked?

Roxburgh Castle had strong defences but Sir James Douglas, Bruce's friend, attacked on Shrove Tuesday when the soldiers were feasting. In the dark Sir James and his men crept up to the walls in single file. Their armour was covered by cloaks. The two men on lookout thought they were cattle. The Scots were able to climb the walls and take everyone by surprise

At Edinburgh Castle Sir Thomas Randolph and thirty daring men climbed the steep cliffs of the castle rock in the dark. One slip would have meant death but once again they took the English soldiers by surprise.

Find:

- **the heavy wooden cart. What is inside?**
- **the weapons being carried.**
- **the cooking pots on the side of the cart.**

At last, in 1313, the only important castle held by the English was at Stirling. Edward II decided that to hold on to Scotland he must save Stirling Castle and force King Robert Bruce to fight in a great battle. He gathered a huge army of 2000 knights and 15,000 spearmen and archers. When 200 wagons full of supplies joined the march it stretched for over three kilometres. These are the kind of wagons he used.

The Battle of Bannockburn

King Robert Bruce had a much smaller army than the English with about 500 horsemen and 5,000 spearmen and archers.

He prepared a plan to attack the English behind the Bannock Burn.

On the road the English horsemen had to cross to get to the castle Bruce put spikes covered with branches and turf.

Find:

◆ **Stirling Castle.**
◆ **the traps on the road. What were they meant to do?**
◆ **Bruce's troops blocking the way to the castle.**

King Edward II decided to take a long way towards Stirling.

Find:

◆ **the road he took along the burn.**
◆ **the marshy ground beside the River Forth.**

Why would this be a bad place for his army to stand?

Edward moved his troops on to firmer ground. This meant the English were now in a very narrow space.

Find:

◆ **Edward's troops.**
◆ **the four Scottish leaders with their troops. Why is Bruce not beside the others?**

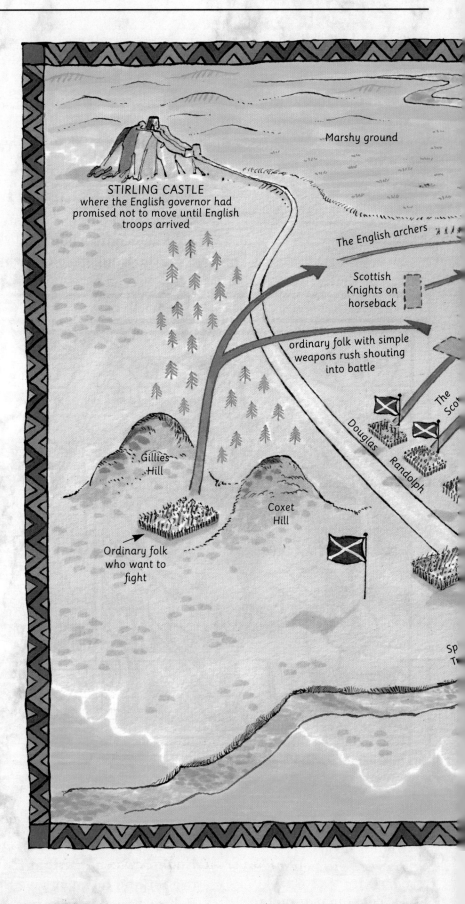

STIRLING CASTLE
where the English governor had promised not to move until English troops arrived

Marshy ground

The English archers

Scottish Knights on horseback

ordinary folk with simple weapons rush shouting into battle

Gillies Hill

Coxet Hill

Douglas

Randolph

The Scot

Ordinary folk who want to fight

Sp T

The battle began at dawn on Midsummer's Day. Each side fired arrows but the English longbows were much better. Edward Bruce, Douglas and Randolph led the Scottish army forward. The English knights were pushed together

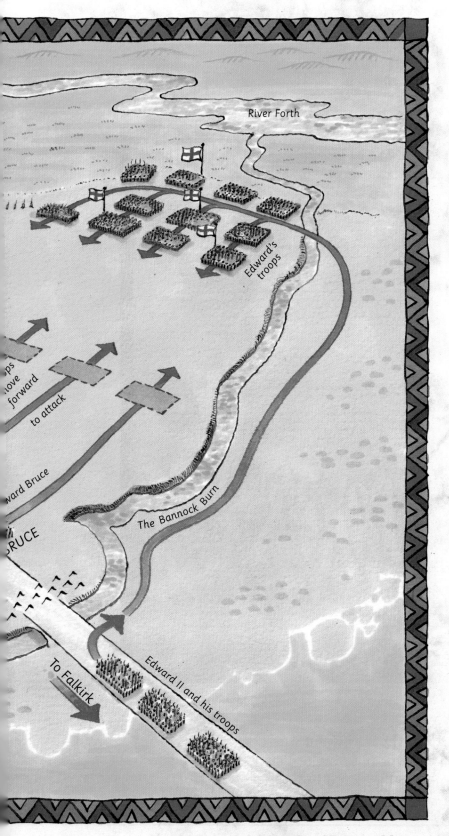

River Forth

Edward's troops

to attack

move forward

...ward Bruce

BRUCE

The Bannock Burn

To Falkirk

Edward II and his troops

A plan of the Battle of Bannockburn

Find:

◆ the Scottish knights on horseback.
◆ the English archers.

Then Bruce moved his own men into the attack. The English were driven back on the streams and marshy pools beside the river.

A little band of ordinary folk who were not really soldiers had been hidden from sight.

Find:

◆ the people between Gillies and Coxet Hill.

When they appeared from the edge of the forest and rushed shouting into battle it was the last blow for Edward. The knights in their heavy armour were trapped in the marshy ground.

Edward had fought bravely but now he was told he should flee. He rode as fast as he could to Dunbar and took a boat for England.

The Scots had won a great victory.

The Battle of Bannockburn made the Scots free from England with a king who had proved that he was fit to be their leader.

between the Bannock Burn and the marsh. They got in one another's way and in the way of the archers. Bruce sent the Scottish knights to charge at the archers and scatter them.

The Declaration of Arbroath

In 1320 Scottish nobles and churchmen met at Arbroath
Abbey to send a very important letter to Pope John XXII,
the head of the Christian Church.

The Declaration of Arbroath

They wanted to make it clear to the Pope that Scotland was
a free country and that the English king was not overlord of
Scotland. It was not until 1328, not long before King Robert
died, that the English at last gave up all claims to Scotland.

The letter is written in Latin, the language of the Church.
It ends by saying:

> For so long as one hundred men remain alive,
> we shall never submit to the rule of the English.
> It is not for glory or riches or honour that we fight but only for
> freedom which no good man will give up except with his life.